# THE WRENCH

## LEARNING ABOUT TOOLS

David and Patricia Armentrout

The Rourke Book Co., Inc.
Vero Beach, Florida 32964

PHOTO CREDITS
© Sears, Roebuck & Co.: cover; © Armentrout: title, pages 10, 17,
21; © IMS: page 7; ©East Coast Studios: pages 4, 8, 12, 13, 15, 18;

ACKNOWLEDGEMENTS
The authors thank the Butler Township Ohio Fire Dept. for their help
in the preparation of this book

**Library of Congress Cataloging-in-Publication Data**

Armentrout, Patricia, 1960-
   The wrench / by Patricia Armentrout and David Armentrout.
      p. cm. — (Learning about tools)
   Includes index.
   ISBN 1-55916-118-3
   1. Wrenches—Juvenile literature.   [1. Wrenches. 2. Tools.]
I. Armentrout, David, 1962-     II. Title. III. Series.
TJ1201.W8A76 1995
621.9' 72—dc20                   94–45590
                                    CIP
                                      AC

**Printed in the USA**

# TABLE OF CONTENTS

# WRENCHES

Wrenches are turning tools. They make it easier to loosen or tighten nuts and bolts. They are made of metal and have a jaw or opening at one or both ends.

Wrenches come in many styles and sizes. Some have **adjustable** (a-JUST-abul), or moveable, jaws. This is so the jaw can be made to fit different sized objects.

The wrench opening or jaw must fit snug around the nut, bolt, or object to be turned.

*It is important that the wrench fits snug around the nut*

# A MECHANIC'S TOOL

Without tools it would be impossible to build the vehicles we use every day. **Mechanics** (mi-KAN-iks) use a variety of tools to build and repair bicycles, boats, motorcycles, and cars.

At an Indy 500 auto race, a pit crew works with wrenches and other tools to keep their driver's car in the race. A fast crew can change all four tires, wash the windows, and fill the gas tank in under 16 seconds! Can you imagine how long it would take without tools?

*A pit crew makes repairs on a car during an auto race*

# COMMON WRENCHES

The open-end wrench is one of the most common wrenches used today. It has a non-adjustable, C-shaped jaw at one or both ends.

The box wrench has an enclosed jaw at one or both ends. It is made to fit completely around a nut or bolt. A combination wrench has a box-end on one side of the handle and an open-end on the other.

The box and open-end wrenches are available in sets that offer many different opening sizes.

*A simple box-end wrench works well for easy car repairs*

# THE CRESCENT WRENCH

The crescent wrench is popular because it is the most useful adjustable wrench.

This wrench has a crescent or C-shaped jaw at one end. The jaw can be adjusted to fit tightly around different size nuts and bolts.

The crescent wrench is made in many sizes. They range from tiny pocket size models to very large wrenches two feet long.

*A crescent wrench can adjust to fit almost any size nut, like the ones used on bicycles*

*Robots, like this one used in tool making, complete jobs that are too dangerous for workers*

*A special wrench called a lug nut wrench is used to loosen and remove the nuts when changing a tire*

# NUTS AND BOLTS

All wrenches are used to apply **torque** (tork), or force, to turn objects. The objects turned are usually nuts and bolts.

A nut is a metal block with a hole in the center. The hole is always round. The outer shape can be square, round, or six-sided. A shape with six sides is called a **hexagon** (HEK-sa-gon).

A bolt is a metal rod. Bolts are made in many sizes that fit different sized nuts. A nut and bolt hold two or more pieces of wood, metal, or other materials together.

*Nuts and bolts are used to hold different materials together*

## A PLUMBER'S TOOL

A pipe wrench is a basic **plumber's** (PLUM-erz) tool. It has a moveable jaw that is lined with teeth, or grooves. When the wrench is turned, the jaw tightens around the pipe.

The monkey wrench is also known as a plumber's tool. It adjusts to fit different sized pipes, but the jaws are smooth instead of grooved.

Sometimes plumbers use one wrench to hold onto a pipe while using another to **fasten** (FAS-en) a metal fitting. A metal fitting is used to attach two pipes together.

*This plumber uses a pipe wrench to tighten a metal fitting*

# THE SOCKET WRENCH

Sockets are made to cover or fit over a nut or bolt head. Socket wrenches are often used in automotive work and are usually purchased as a set.

A basic set might have three **universal** (U-na-VER-sul) drives, or handles, a dozen or more socket sizes, and several **extenders** (ex-TEND-erz). Extenders are attachments that lengthen the reach of the wrench.

To use the socket wrench, the proper size socket is fitted to the chosen handle. The socket is then placed on the nut or bolt and turned.

*A socket wrench used with an extender makes bolts in difficult places easy to reach*

19

## SPECIAL WRENCHES

Have you ever wondered how a firefighter opens a fire hydrant? They use a hydrant wrench. The hydrant wrench is used to open the valve so a hose can be attached.

To attach a hose to the fire department's pumper truck, firefighters use a spanner wrench. The spanner wrench is made to adjust to different size hoses.

Today, almost every town is served by a fire department. Without the special tools they use, it would be very hard for firefighters to protect their community.

*This firefighter uses a hydrant wrench to open a valve on a fire hydrant*

# PROPER TOOL USE

Accidents are never expected, but could happen at any time. An adult should be there to help and teach children good safety habits.

A wrench that is in poor condition, or has a jaw opening that is too large, can damage a nut or bolt by rounding off its edges. Always choose the correct size wrench for the job.

Correct use and proper care of wrenches and other tools will make working with tools fun and safe.

# Glossary

**adjustable** (a-JUST-abul) — can be made to fit

**extenders** (ex-TEND-erz) — objects that can be attached to other objects to make them longer

**fasten** (FAS-en) — to attach or hold together

**hexagon** (HEK-sa-gon) — having six sides, six angles

**mechanics** (mi-KAN-iks) — people who repair machines or engines

**plumbers** (PLUM-erz) — people who work on or repair gas and water pipes

**torque** (tork) — a force that produces rotation

**universal** (U-na-VER-sul) — for use among all

# INDEX